DATE DUE MAR 0 7

Mosquito

Heather L. Miller

KIDHAVEN
PRESS™

THOMSON
━━━━━━★━━━━━━ ™
GALE

San Diego • Detroit • New York • San Francisco • Cleveland
New Haven, Conn. • Waterville, Maine • London • Munich

THOMSON

™

GALE

LIBRARY OF CONGRESS CATALOGING-IN-PUBLICATION DATA

Miller, Heather, L.
  Mosquito / by Heather L. Miller.
    p. cm.—(Bugs)
Summary: Describes the physical characteristics, behavior, and habitat of mosquitoes.
Includes bibliographical references and index.
  ISBN 0-7377-1772-6 (alk. paper)
1. Mosquitoes—Juvenile literature. [1. Mosquitoes.] I. Title. II. Series.
  QL536.M56 2004
  595 .77'2—dc22

2003013871

Printed in China

CONTENTS

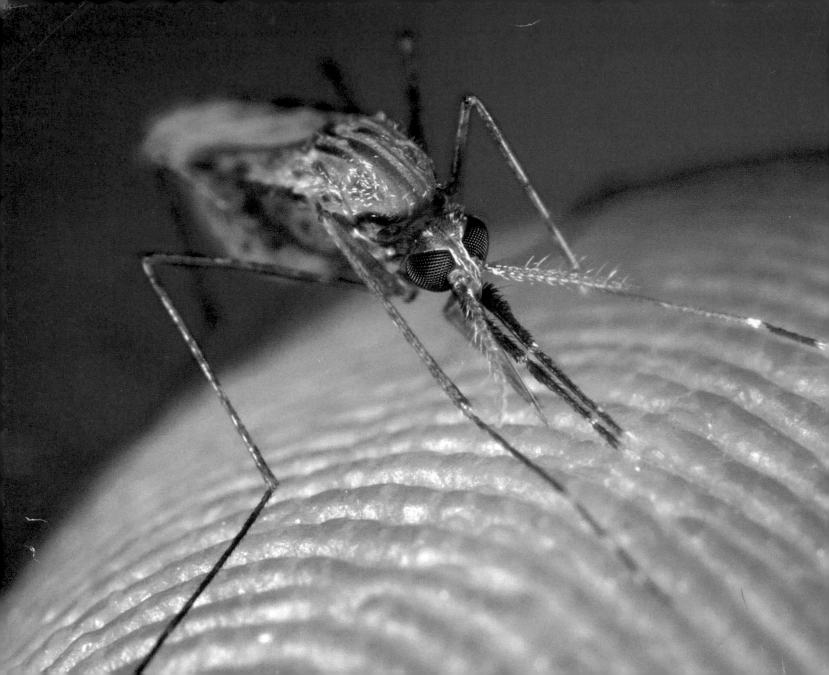

Little Fly

For the past 50 million years, mosquitoes have swarmed the earth. Today, nearly three thousand different species of mosquitoes can be found zipping through bustling cities, over dry deserts, across the Arctic tundra, in rain forests, and even at the tops of small mountains. Mosquitoes have been found on every continent in the world but Antarctica.

Opposite: Mosquitoes have swarmed the earth for millions of years.

Scientists have recorded almost two hundred different mosquito species living in North America. In the United States, the warm, moist climate of Florida provides an ideal habitat for seventy-seven different species. Some mosquitoes prefer cooler temperatures. One type of *Aedes* mosquito thrives in the Canadian Arctic. The small fly known as the mosquito is a familiar neighbor to almost every creature on earth.

The word mosquito means "little fly." It is a fitting description since the mosquito is typically the size of a sesame seed. But a few types are larger. The American gallinipper is a king-sized mosquito with a body that is almost one inch long.

Lots of Lenses

The mosquito's body is made up of three sections, including the head, thorax, and abdomen. The mosquito's small, round head is nearly covered by two **compound eyes**. Each compound eye is made up of thousands of lenses. Each lens works independently, allowing the mosquito to look in many directions at the same time.

Even though the mosquito is equipped with specialized eyes, it cannot see clearly. The mosquito uses its eyes to sense movements. With so many lenses looking in so many directions, the mosquito can sense a swatting hand in plenty of time to fly to safety.

While the mosquito uses its compound eyes to see, it depends on its two **antennae** to hear and smell. Tiny hairs grow along the shaft of each antenna. The mosquito uses these hairs to pick up important information such as sound vibrations.

The hairs along the mosquito's antennae also provide scientists with important information. Through a magnifying glass, a male mosquito's antennae appear wispy and feather-like, while a female mosquito has antennae covered with short, stout hairs. Equipped with sensory organs such as antennae and compound eyes, the mosquito's head serves as the insect's information center.

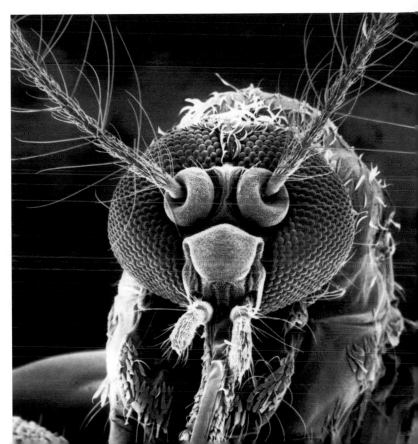

Mosquitoes use their compound eyes to sense movement and their hairy antennae to hear and smell.

The mosquito's head is connected to the thorax. Tiny, colored scales cover the thorax. Most mosquitoes are brown, black, tan, or gray. Other mosquitoes have variations such as stripes or spots. Some mosquitoes have **iridescent** scales, making them appear shiny green or bright blue.

Wing Power

Scales also cover the mosquito's wings. The high-pitched humming sound heard when a mosquito is near is actually the sound of its wings flapping. A mosquito beats its wings almost one thousand times per second. The mosquito must flap its wings constantly to keep the weight of its body in the air.

The longest and heaviest section of the mosquito's body is the abdomen. The abdomen looks a bit like a grain of rice. Eight pairs of **spiracles**, or air holes, line the abdomen. Air flows into the spiracles and passes through small tubes that carry oxygen to every part of the mosquito's body.

Tiny scales cover the mosquito's wings.

1 Compound eyes, made up of thousands of tiny lenses, sense movement. Two hairy antennae help the mosquito hear and smell.

2 Tiny colored scales cover the mosquito's wings and body. Powerful wings flap at a rate of one thousand beats per second.

3 Long, tubelike mouth, or proboscis, slurps up food. The female mosquito uses her proboscis to suck blood from animals and people.

Body of a Mosquito

The mosquito's three-part body design is simple yet efficient. This design helps the mosquito thrive all over the world.

The Life Cycle

Opposite: Female mosquitoes lay from one hundred to three hundred eggs (inset) at a time.

Every mosquito undergoes a four-step **metamorphosis**, or change. During each stage, the mosquito changes until it reaches maturity as a fully developed, adult mosquito.

The mosquito life cycle begins with an egg. Depending on the species, female mosquitoes lay from one hundred to three hundred eggs in a single batch. Some females deposit one egg at a time into

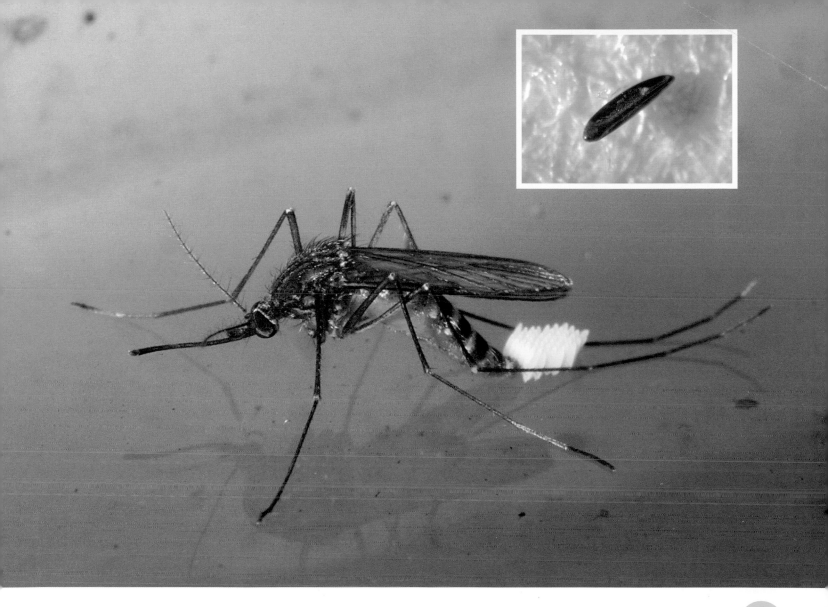

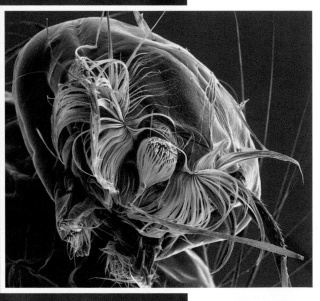

Wormlike larvae (left) hatch from floating eggs. Below, a larva face is shown enlarged eighty-five times its normal size.

either water or moist soil. Other mosquitoes group their eggs together in **egg rafts**. The rafts float on the water's surface until the eggs are ready to open.

Wriggly Worms

Most mosquito eggs begin to hatch about two days after they are laid. Tiny wormlike creatures, called **larvae**, emerge from the eggs. The larvae live in water but must also breathe fresh air. Most mosquito larvae use a special tube, called a **siphon**, to help them breathe. The siphon tube is a lot like a diver's snorkel. The siphon stays level with the water's surface while the larva hangs upside down, under the water, where it pulls air into its body through the siphon.

Sometimes a larva must leave the surface and dive deep into the water. When a mosquito larva senses danger, it begins to thrash in an S-shaped motion. By doing this, the larva can swim down to safety. Mosquito larvae are often called "wrigglers" because of the way they wriggle away from danger.

A mosquito larva also wriggles to gather food. As the larva passes through the water, mouth brushes pull in bits of food such as bacteria, protozoa, and small plant particles. A mosquito larva eats frequently to help it grow quickly.

As the mosquito larva grows, the thin, protective shell surrounding its body becomes tight. The shell splits, and a larger, more mature larva crawls out. This process is called **molting**. A mosquito larva will molt four times in about ten days.

Great Changes

After its final molt, the larva curls up, grows a thicker shell, and slips into a resting state. During this time, the young mosquito is called a **pupa**. The pupa does not eat. It only moves to escape danger and gather air from the surface.

Although the pupa may appear to be inactive, great changes are taking place inside its protective shell. In about one to four days, the pupa will rise to the surface of the water, split its shell, and emerge as a fully grown, adult mosquito.

Before a new mosquito can fly, it must wait for all of its body parts to dry. As the mosquito's body dries, it becomes hard. Once the mosquito's wings

A mosquito pupa squeezes out of its shell before emerging as an adult.

Mosquito

are stable, it can fly away to look for food and a mate.

A male mosquito finds his mate by listening for the sound vibrations given off by females. With his antennae, the male mosquito can determine whether a mosquito is a female by the high-pitched vibrations given off by her beating wings. A male mosquito must find a mate quickly. The average male mosquito lives only seven to ten days.

Most female mosquitoes live much longer than males. A female mosquito can expect to live about thirty days. Some females have been known to live as long as five months. From the egg stage to adulthood, the mosquito lives a short, but active, life.

The male mosquito finds a mate by listening for the female's beating wings. Here, a mosquito pair mates.

Homeless Insect

Because most mosquitoes have a very short life they do not need permanent shelters the way some insects do. Tall grasses and hollow logs provide the protection mosquitoes need from strong winds, heavy rains, and cool temperatures. Where mosquitoes live is dictated by their constant work in mating and laying eggs.

Water Lover

All mosquitoes breed and lay eggs near water. The types of water mosquitoes choose can be broken into four categories: **running water, transient water, permanent water,** and **container water.**

Sources of running water include streams, creeks, and small rivers. Mosquitoes that live near running water are most commonly found in the tropical regions of South America and Africa. Mosquitoes and larvae living in rivers and streams tend to stay near the water's edge where the currents are less powerful. Near the riverbank, larvae and egg-laying adults cling to weeds and grasses to avoid being swept away by rushing water.

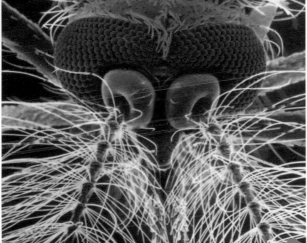

All mosquitoes live and breed near water (above). Here, a mosquito head has been magnified two hundred twenty times its normal size.

Other mosquitoes prefer water that does not move. Some of these mosquitoes search for transient, or temporary, water sources. Transient water areas are not always filled with water. After a heavy rain or snow melt, ditches, snow pools, and flood-

Mosquito larvae (above) mature in a jar of rainwater (left). Some mosquitoes prefer transient, or temporary, sources of water.

plains fill with water, creating pools and small ponds. These areas dry up as the water evaporates. With the next rain, they will fill with water again.

Some mosquito eggs, such as those laid by the *Aedes* mosquito, need to be soaked and dried several times before they are ready to hatch. The wet and dry cycles found in transient water areas provide ideal breeding conditions for the *Aedes* mosquito.

Permanent Water Sources

Swamps and ponds provide mosquitoes with another type of nonmoving water. Because swamps and ponds always contain water, they are classified as permanent water sources. Cattails, sedges, and rushes grow alongside ponds and provide mosquitoes with shelter.

While a pond provides the mosquito with shelter and an ideal breeding area, the deep waters found there are not necessary. Mosquitoes can breed in small amounts of water. Many mosquitoes seek out container water to foster their eggs. Water collected in plant leaves, flowerpots, rotting logs, and even elephant footprints can support a batch of mosquito larvae.

Tiny House Guest

Mosquitoes stay busy breeding during the warm seasons, but they cannot survive the extremely cold conditions of winter. Some adult mosquitoes seek shelter when temperatures drop. The house mosquito hides out in warm houses during cold

During the cold winter some mosquitoes make their homes in the burrows of small animals such as this muskrat.

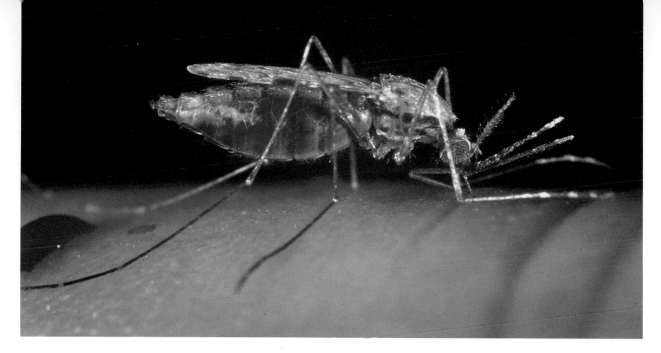

weather. The house mosquito tucks itself between walls and in basements where it hibernates through the winter and emerges in spring.

Other types of mosquitoes hibernate in natural shelters. Sleeping muskrats, mice, and other burrowing animals frequently share their warm homes with mosquitoes.

Whether searching for wet breeding grounds or crawling into a warm home for the winter, mosquitoes are experts at adapting to a wide variety of habitats.

Mosquitoes are experts at adapting to different habitats.

Mosquito Menu

Opposite: Thousands of hungry mosquitoes, like this one filled with blood, swarm the sky in search of their next meal.

osquitoes are low-ranking members of the food chain. They are scooped up as snacks by many creatures. As larvae, mosquitoes risk being gobbled up by fish, water beetles, and dragonflies. Birds, bats, spiders, frogs, moles, and most any other small animal with a grumbling stomach hunt the meatier adult mosquitoes.

When the mosquito's stomach is empty, it searches for the nearest flowerbed. Flower juice, or **nectar**, gives the mosquito the energy it needs to fly. While all mosquitoes depend on the nutrition gathered from the sugar in flowers, only female mosquitoes seek out blood meals.

The female mosquito requires a protein-rich meal to help her eggs develop properly. Blood is rich in protein and an abundant supply can be found in almost every living creature.

Liquid Lunch

Whether it is nectar or blood on the menu, female mosquitoes suck

The female mosquito uses her long proboscis (right) and sharp stylets (below) to stab victims and suck out their blood.

up their liquid lunches through a special type of mouthpart called a **proboscis**. The proboscis is a long and slender tube. Inside the proboscis are six needlelike parts called **stylets**. When a female mosquito attacks, it stabs its victim with four of the stylets. The mosquito's **saliva** flows into the victim's wound to prevent the blood from clotting, or becoming thick. A suction pump brings blood in through the remaining two stylets and up to the mosquito's head. A second suction pump pulls the blood into the mosquito's gut.

As the mosquito drinks, its gut expands like a water balloon. Mosquitoes often pull in enough blood to more than double their own size. That is like an 80-pound child sitting down to eat lunch and leaving the table weighing 160 pounds.

After taking a meal, the mosquito leaves behind an itchy reminder of its visit. The mosquito's saliva often irritates the skin of its victim, causing a red, raised welt. Luckily most mosquitoes take the blood they need and leave their victims behind with only a few itchy bumps.

Hungry Attacker

Some species of mosquitoes are vicious attackers. One type of *Aedes* mosquito found in the Canadian Arctic is known

After drinking blood, mosquitoes can swell to twice their normal size.

Some species of mosquitoes are very aggressive, like this one shown magnified two hundred sixty-four times.

for its aggressive behavior. Because the warm season is short in the Canadian Arctic, the mosquitoes that live there have little time to collect food and breed. The *Aedes* fly together in huge, hungry swarms. An animal unlucky enough to come across such a swarm could be bitten up to nine thousand times per minute. This species of *Aedes* is so desperate for food they sometimes feed off of dead animals. Thick blankets of these mosquitoes have been found feeding off of the carcasses of caribou and other animals.

The mosquito is a delicious treat for many creatures, but the biting insect is also pesky and sometimes aggressive. Wherever creatures roam, the mosquito can most likely be found nearby, waiting to slurp up its next meal.

GLOSSARY

antennae: Thin organs growing out from between the mosquito's eyes used to gather sensory information.

compound eyes: Eyes made up of thousands of units, or lenses.

container water: Water collected in a container.

egg raft: A bundle of mosquito eggs that floats on water.

iridescent: A play of colors producing a rainbow effect.

larvae: Wormlike forms that hatch from a mosquito egg.

metamorphosis: A change in physical form from egg to adult mosquito.

molt: To shed an outer shell or covering.

nectar: A sugary liquid secreted by flowers.

permanent water: A body of water that is always present.

proboscis: A long, tubelike, sucking mouthpart.

pupa: The stage in metamorphosis between the larva and adult stage.

running water: Water that flows.

saliva: A clear liquid secreted from the mouth.

siphon: A tube through which a mosquito larva breathes.

spiracles: Holes through which a mosquito sucks in air.

stylet: A long, slender, piercing mouthpart inside the proboscis.

transient water: A temporary body of water.

FOR FURTHER EXPLORATION

Books

Jennifer Coldrey and George Bernard, *Mosquito.* Morristown, NJ: Silver Burdett Press, 1997. This book from the Stopwatch series includes colorful photos of the life cycle of the mosquito.

Ann Matthews, *My First Pocket Guide to Insects.* Washington, DC: National Geographic, 1996. Inside this easy-to-read book are photographs, descriptions, and fun facts describing many insects.

Cari Meister, *Mosquitoes.* Edina, MN: ABDO, 2001. Part of the Checkerboard Science and Nature Library, this book tells about what mosquitoes eat, where they live, and how they relate to humans.

Websites

The American Mosquito Control Association (www.mosquito.org). Click on "mosquito information" to reveal detailed facts describing every aspect of the mosquito.

How Stuff Works (www.howstuff works.com). The article "How Mosquitoes Work" provides an abundance of information as well as clear, close-up photographs of mosquitoes in action.

University of Arizona (www.in sected.arizona.edu). Look for the information sheet on mosquitoes to reveal diagrams and general information including paragraphs describing both the positive and negative effects of mosquitoes on the ecosystem.

INDEX

PICTURE CREDITS

ABOUT THE AUTHOR

Heather Miller has written more than a dozen books for young readers along with a wide range of educational materials for elementary grade teachers. She grew up in Minnesota where she spent her summer evenings scratching dozens of mosquito bites. Today Ms. Miller lives in Indiana with her husband and two daughters where she enjoys teaching art and writing for children.